Kay Gardiner and Ann Shayne

xo
Kay

xx
Ann

2. Introduction

6. **Calligraphy Cardigan**

18. Revolution in the Round

20. **Ironworks Beret**

28. **Liberty Tree Pullover**

38. "Hope" is the thing with feathers

40. **Elaine's Capelet**

48. Getting to Know Designer Norah Gaughan

50. Abbreviations

52. A Daily Dose of MDK

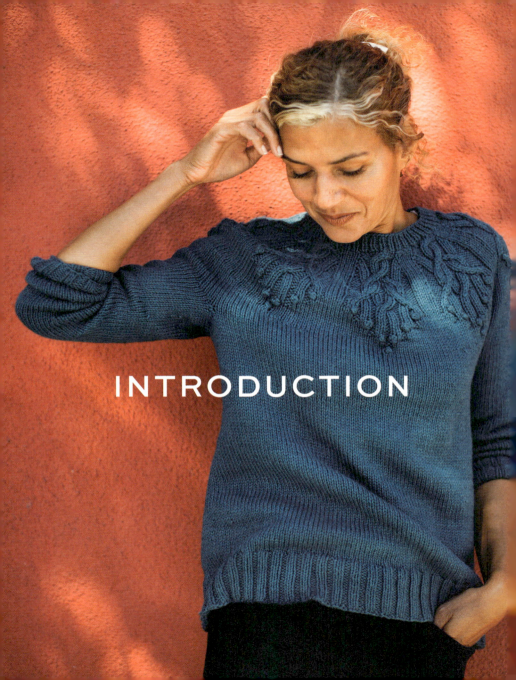

# INTRODUCTION

THE EARTH SPINS, one revolution every day of the week, and so do we, along for the ride, unaware that we're on the move, thousands of miles, even as we slurp our coffee and dream of Friday.

When we think of revolution, we think of all sorts of things. A Ferris wheel, a merry go round. A toddler discovering what it is to spin and spin until she falls down, laughing. A Beatles song. Round trips, a cakewalk, a walk in the park. There's something comforting about returning to where we started.

But sometimes, a turn of thinking takes us far from where we began. A new idea. A new order.

The opportunity to leave behind what's old and broken. The risk of doing that. The risk of not doing it.

Crossing the Delaware, "When the beating of your heart echoes the beating of the drums. . . ."

We feel so lucky to have a whole Field Guide of designs by Norah Gaughan. For more than 30 years, Norah has set our minds awhirl. She is a genius of construction, a master of cables, and a fearless innovator. She is a true revolutionary.

Knitting is often worked in the round, in circles that go and go until we arrive at a finished piece that seems impossible to have emerged from a simple rhythm of knit and purl.

This is what we have in the four designs that Norah Gaughan gives us. Her inspiration is revolution in all its forms. The twists of a tree, the ironwork of the Eiffel Tower, a curl of calligraphy.

Three of these cable motifs are fully interchangeable, making it possible to mix and match pattern and garment as you like. Freedom to choose—such a Norah Gaughan idea.

Of course, when it comes to revolution, the place we end up is not always where we expected. And while that can make life awfully challenging, revolution in knitting is a much simpler thing: it makes for an extraordinary ride.

You say you want a revolution? Well you know, we'd all love to change the world. In the meantime, we knit on, through all crises, with hope in our hearts no matter what.

Love,

*Kay   Ann*

*The cables Norah designed for the (top to bottom) Calligraphy Cardigan, Elaine's Capelet, and Liberty Tree Pullover are all worked in the round at the same gauge—20 stitches × 28 rows = 4" (10 cm) in stockinette stitch—so are interchangeable.*

# CALLIGRAPHY CARDIGAN

*Design by*

Norah Gaughan

**A** CAP SLEEVE ON A CARDIGAN? Aren't cardigans supposed to have sleeves? It's a sleeve revolution, people! Rise up and leave behind the cuffs that bind you!

Once again, Norah Gaughan gives us a new way of thinking about the garments we make. The short sleeve here means we can layer this with a T-shirt, long sleeved or short. Or we can wear it as is.

The cables show us Norah playing with circles and curves, creating a yoke that looks as much like a calligraphy doodle as a knitting pattern. The scale here is big—a juicy, dimensional design that is probably not like any cable you've worked.

The yarn is Merino DK from Periwinkle Sheep, a soft wool that color wizard Karin Maag-Tanchak dyed in nine exquisite shades for this project and exclusively for MDK. Choosing just one color from this palette seems an impossibility for us, so we might just need multiples of this versatile cardi. See all of the color possibilities on pages 16–17.

## KNITTED MEASUREMENTS

- Bust: 33½ (37½, 41½, 45½, 49½, 53½, 57½)" [85 (95.5, 105.5, 115.5, 125.5, 136, 146) cm], buttoned
- Length: 21 (22, 22½, 23½, 24, 25, 25½)" [53.5 (56, 57, 59.5, 61, 63.5, 65) cm]

## SIZE

To fit bust sizes 28–30 (32–34, 36–38, 40–42, 44–46, 48–50, 52–54)" [71–76 (81.5–86.5, 91.5–96.5, 101.5–106.5, 112–117, 122–127, 132–137) cm]

## MATERIALS

- Merino DK by Periwinkle Sheep [100 g skeins, each approx 225 yds (205 m), 100% superwash merino]: 4 (4, 5, 6, 7, 7, 8) skeins Hydrangea or any of 9 colors shown on pages 16–17.
- Size US 7 (4.5 mm) circular needle, 24" (60 cm) long or longer, or size needed to achieve gauge
- Size US 5 (3.75 mm) circular needle, 24" (60 cm) or longer, and double-pointed needles (set of 4 or 5)
- Stitch markers
- Cable needle
- Waste yarn
- 7 buttons, ½" (15 mm) diameter

## GAUGE

20 sts and 28 rows = 4" (10 cm) over stockinette stitch, using larger needle

## NOTES

Cardigan is worked from top down to arm-holes, then sleeves and body are divided and worked separately to bottom edge. Short rows are used to shape back neck. Place markers between Cable Pattern repeats to track position in pattern.

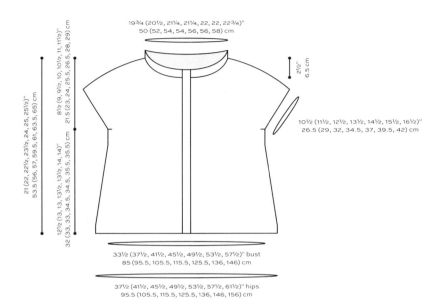

## CABLE PATTERN

(multiple of 14 sts + 1; inc to multiple of 28 sts + 1; inc 2 sts per rep on RS on Rows 3–11, 15 and 19); *Note:* See abbreviations and chart on pages 14–15.

— *Row 1 (RS):* P1, *p1, k3, p5, k3, p2; rep from * to end.
— *Row 2 and all WS Rows:* Knit the knit sts and purl the purl sts as they face you; knit yos tbl.
— *Row 3:* P1, *p1, k1, M1L, k2, p5, k2, M1R, k1, p2; rep from * to end.
— *Row 5:* P1, *yo, p1, 4/2 LPC, p1, 4/2 RPC, p1, yo, p1; rep from * to end.
— *Row 7:* P1, *yo, p4, 4/1/4 RPC, p4, yo, p1; rep from * to end.
— *Row 9:* P1, *yo, p2, 4/3 RC, p1, 4/3 LC, p2, yo, p1; rep from * to end.
— *Row 11:* P1, *yo, p1, 4/2 RPC, k3, p1, k3, 4/2 LPC, p1, yo, p1; rep from * to end.
— *Row 13:* P1, *p1, 4/1 RPC, p2, 3/1/3 RPC, p2, 4/1 LPC, p2; rep from * to end.

- *Row 15*: P1, *yo, p1, k4, p3, k3, p1, k3, p3, k4, p1, yo, p1; rep from * to end.
- *Row 17*: Rep Row 2.
- *Row 19*: P1, *yo, p2, k4, p3, 3/1/3 RPC, p3, k4, p2, yo, p1; rep from * to end.
- *Rows 21 and 23*: Rep Row 2.
- *Row 25*: P1, *p3, 4/1 LPC, p2, 3/1/3 RPC, p2, 4/1 RPC, p4; rep from * to end.
- *Row 27*: P1, *p4, 4/2 LPC, k3, p1, k3, 4/2 RPC, p5; rep from * to end.
- *Row 29*: P1, *p6, 4/3 LPC, p1, 4/3 RPC, p7; rep from * to end.
- *Row 31*: P1, *p9, 4/1/4 RPC, p10; rep from * to end.
- *Row 33*: P1, *p6, 4/3 RC, k1, 4/3 LC, p7; rep from * to end.
- *Row 35*: P1, *p4, 4/2 RC, k7, 4/2 LC, p5; rep from * to end.
- *Row 37*: P1, *p2, 4/2 RC, k11, 4/2 LC, p3; rep from * to end.
- *Row 39*: P1, *p1, 4/1 RC, k15, 4/1 LC, p2; rep from * to end.
- *Row 41*: P1, *4/1 RC, k17, 4/1 LC, p1; rep from * to end.
- *Row 43*: P1, *3/1 RC, k19, 3/1 LC, p1; rep from * to end.
- *Row 45*: P1, *2/1 RC, k21, 2/1 LC, p1; rep from * to end.
- *Row 47*: P1, *1/1 RC, k23, 1/1 LC, p1; rep from * to end.

## YOKE

- Using larger circular needle, CO 99 (113, 127, 141, 155, 169, 183) sts.
- Work Rows 1-47 of Cable Pattern, working incs as indicated—197 (225, 253, 281, 309, 337, 365) sts. Pm 42 sts in from each edge.
- Change to st st.

### SHAPE BACK NECK

- *Short Row 1 (RS)*: Knit to second marker, remove marker, turn.
- *Short Row 2 (WS)*: DS, purl to marker, remove marker, turn.
- *Short Row 3*: DS, knit to DS, close DS, k3, turn.
- *Short Row 4*: DS, purl to DS, close DS, p3, turn.
- *Short Rows 5-18*: Rep Short Rows 3 and 4 seven times.
- *Short Row 19*: DS, knit to DS, close DS, knit to end.
- Purl 1 row, closing DS when you come to it.
- *Inc Row (RS)*: K7 (8, 7, 14, 11, 28, 20), M1L, [k14 (16, 14, 28, 22, 56, 36), M1L] 13 (13, 17, 9, 13, 5, 9) times, knit to end—211 (239, 271, 291, 323, 343, 375) sts.

— Continuing in st st, work even until piece is 8½ (9, 9½, 10, 10½, 11, 11½)" [21.5 (23, 24, 25.5, 26.5, 28, 29) cm] from highest point, ending with a WS row.

## BODY

— *Dividing Row (RS)*: K34 (39, 44, 48, 53, 57, 62), place next 38 (42, 48, 50, 56, 58, 64) sts on waste yarn for right armhole, CO 6 (6, 6, 7, 7, 8, 8) sts for underarm, pm for side, CO 7 (7, 7, 8, 8, 9, 9) sts for underarm, k67 (77, 87, 95, 105, 113, 123), place next 38 (42, 48, 50, 56, 58, 64) sts on waste yarn for left armhole, CO 7 (7, 7, 8, 8, 9, 9) sts for underarm, pm for side, CO 6 (6, 6, 7, 7, 8, 8) sts for underarm, knit to end—161 (181, 201, 221, 241, 261, 281) sts.
— Work in st st until piece measures 2" [5 cm] from underarm, ending with a WS row.

SHAPE HIPS
— *Inc Row (RS)*: [Knit to 2 sts before marker, M1R, k2, sm, k2, M1L] twice, knit to end—4 sts inc.
— Rep Inc Row every 2" (5 cm) 4 more times—181 (201, 221, 241, 261, 281, 301) sts.
— Work even until piece measures 11½ (12, 12, 12½, 12½, 13, 13)" [29 (30.5, 30.5, 32, 32, 33, 33) cm] from underarm, ending with a WS row.

Special Technique
*German Short Rows*: Work the number of stitches indicated in the pattern, turn work. With the yarn in front, slip the first stitch purlwise, then pull the yarn tightly up and over the needle so that the two legs of the stitch below the slipped stitch are showing; this creates a Double Stitch (DS) on the right needle. If the next stitch to be worked is a purl stitch, bring the yarn back around to the front, ready to purl; if the next stitch is a knit stitch, keep the yarn to the back, ready to knit.

When you come to the gap created by the DS on the next row, knit or purl the two legs of the DS together to close the DS, depending on whether the stitch is to be a knit stitch or a purl stitch. The two legs of the DS will always be counted as a single stitch.

- Change to smaller circular needle.
- *Inc Row:* *K5, M1L; rep from * to last 6 sts, knit to end—216 (240, 264, 288, 312, 336, 360) sts.
- *Row 1:* K3, *p2, k2; rep from * to last st, k1.
- *Row 2:* Knit the knit sts and purl the purl sts as they face you.
- Work even until ribbing measures 1" (2.5 cm), ending with a WS row.
- Knit 1 row.
- BO all sts purlwise.

RIGHT ARMHOLE EDGING
- Using smaller dpns, and beg at center underarm, pick up and knit 7 (7, 7, 8, 8, 9, 9) sts from the 6 (6, 6, 7, 7, 8, 8) CO underarm sts, knit across sts from waste yarn, pick up and knit 8 (8, 8, 9, 9, 10, 10) sts from the 7 (7, 7, 8, 8, 9, 9) CO underarm sts—53 (57, 63, 67, 73, 77, 83) sts; pm for beg of rnd and work in the rnd as follows:
- Purl 2 rnds.
- BO all sts purlwise.

LEFT ARMHOLE EDGING
- Using smaller dpns, and beg at center underarm, pick up and knit 8 (8, 8, 9, 9, 10, 10) sts from the 7 (7,

7, 8, 8, 9, 9) CO underarm sts, knit across sts from waste yarn, pick up and knit 7 (7, 7, 8, 8, 9, 9) sts from the 6 (6, 6, 7, 7, 8, 8) CO underarm sts—53 (57, 63, 67, 73, 77, 83) sts; pm for beg of rnd and work in the rnd as follows:
- Purl 2 rnds.
- BO all sts purlwise.

FINISHING
**Neckband**
- With RS facing, using smaller circular needle, pick up and knit 92 (96, 100, 100, 104, 104, 108) sts around CO edge [approx 13 (12, 11, 10, 9, 9, 8) sts per Cable Pattern rep].
- *Row 1 (WS):* K3, *p2, k2; rep from * to last st, k1.
- *Row 2:* Knit the knit sts and purl the purl sts as they face you.
- Work even until ribbing measures ¾" (2 cm), ending with a WS row.
- Knit 1 row.
- BO all sts purlwise.

**Button Band**
- With RS facing, using smaller circular needle, pick up and knit 110 (118, 122, 126, 130, 134, 138) sts along left front edge.

- *Row 1 (WS)*: K2, *p2, k2; rep from * to end.
- *Row 2*: K1, p1, *k2, p2; rep from * to last 2 sts, p1, k1.
- Rep Rows 1 and 2 until ribbing measures 1" (2.5 cm), ending with a WS row.
- Knit 1 row.
- BO all sts knitwise. Pm for 7 buttons along button band, the first and last ¾" (2 cm) from top and bottom edges, and the remaining 5 evenly spaced between.

## Buttonhole Band

Work as for button band, working buttonholes on Rows 4 and 5 as follows:

- *Row 4 (RS)*: [Work in pattern to marker, work twice into next st (kfb if next st is a knit st; pfb if next st is a purl st), work 1 st, pass second st over first st to BO 1 st, BO next 2 sts] 7 times, work to end.
- *Row 5*: [Work to buttonhole, turn; CO 3 sts using cable CO, turn; sl last CO st to left needle, work 2 sts tog (k2tog if second st is a knit st, p2tog if second st is a purl st] 7 times, work to end.
- Complete as for button band.
- Weave in ends; block as desired.

## CALLIGRAPHY CARDIGAN CABLE & ABBREVIATION GUIDE

**1/1 LC (1 over 1 Left Cross):** Slip the next st to cn and hold at front of work, k1, k1 from cn.

**1/1 RC (1 over 1 Right Cross):** Slip the next st to cn and hold at back of work, k1, k1 from cn.

**2/1 LC (2 over 1 Left Cross):** Slip the next 2 sts to cn and hold at front of work, k1, k2 from cn.

**2/1 RC (2 over 1 Right Cross):** Slip the next st to cn and hold at back of work, k2, k1 from cn.

**3/1 LC (3 over 1 Left Cross):** Slip the next 3 sts to cn and hold at front of work, k1, k3 from cn.

**3/1 RC (3 over 1 Right Cross):** Slip the next st to cn and hold at back of work, k3, k1 from cn.

**3/1/3 RPC (3 over 1 over 3 Right Purl Cross):** Slip the next 4 sts to cn and hold at back of work, k3, slip the last st from cn to left needle, p1, k3 from cn.

**4/1 LC (4 over 1 Left Cross):** Slip the next 4 sts to cn and hold at front of work, k1, k4 from cn.

**4/1 LPC (4 over 1 Left Purl Cross):** Slip the next 4 sts to cn and hold at front of work, p1, k4 from cn.

**4/1 RC (4 over 1 Right Cross):** Slip the next st to cn and hold at back of work, k4, k1 from cn.

**4/1 RPC (4 over 1 Right Purl Cross):** Slip the next st to cn and hold at back of work, k4, p1 from cn.

**4/1/4 RPC (4 over 1 over 4 Right Purl Cross):** Slip the next 5 sts to cn and hold at back of work, k4, slip the last st from cn to left needle, p1, k4 from cn.

**4/2 LC (4 over 2 Left Cross):** Slip the next 4 sts to cn and hold at front of work, k2, k4 from cn.

**4/2 LPC (4 over 2 Left Purl Cross):** Slip the next 4 sts to cn and hold at front of work, p2, k4 from cn.

**4/2 RC (4 over 2 Right Cross):** Slip the next 2 sts to cn and hold at back of work, k4, k2 from cn.

**4/2 RPC (4 over 2 Right Purl Cross):** Slip the next 2 sts to cn and hold at back of work, k4, p2 from cn.

**4/3 LC (4 over 3 Left Cross):** Slip the next 4 sts to cn and hold at front of work, k3, k4 from cn.

**4/3 LPC (4 over 3 Left Purl Cross):** Slip the next 4 sts to cn and hold at front of work, p3, k4 from cn.

**4/3 RC (4 over 3 Right Cross):** Slip the next 3 sts to cn and hold at back of work, k4, k3 from cn.

**4/3 RPC (4 over 3 Right Purl Cross):** Slip the next 2 sts to cn and hold at back of work, k4, p3 from cn.

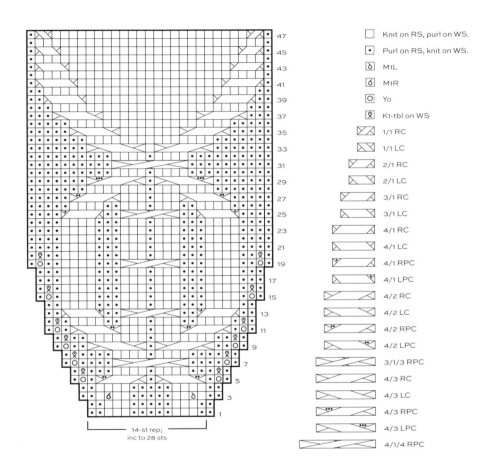

*Periwinkle Sheep DK colors on pages 16–17:* 1. *Pine Forest* 2. *Ballet* 3. *Hydrangea* 4. *Olive* 5. *Geranium* 6. *Dove* 7. *Bisque* 8. *Cadet* 9. *Beaujolais*

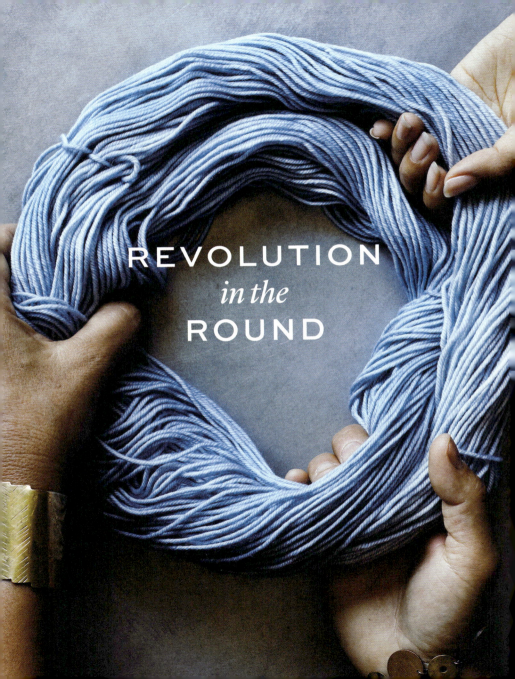

**P**EOPLE ALWAYS ASSUME that somebody who has been knitting as long as I have, and knits as constantly and as publicly as I do, surely must have a knitting circle. Well, I do, and it's about five minutes old. This is how it began.

A year ago, I donated a "knit night at Kay's" to a silent auction for my synagogue, and a group of ten women who knew me or knew of me, and didn't want to see me suffer the shame of my auction donation going unsold, clubbed together and made a joint bid that won the thing. A month or so later, I made them dinner, sent my hypervigilant terrier off on a playdate with a calming golden retriever as nanny, and the group appeared, a gang of knitters ranging from utter newcomers to old hands.

It was so much fun that at the end of the evening, I proposed to these women: Could we do this again? Would they be my knitting circle? Yes, yes, they would. And they are. And it's a beautiful thing.

Sometimes revolution is quiet. It takes the form of a human circle, friends, some new, some old, all laying down stitches together. Sometimes we talk about the change we want to see in the world. Sometimes we become the change we want to see in the world.

—Kay

# IRONWORKS BERET

*Design by*

Norah Gaughan

CAN SOMETHING AS SMALL AND ORDINARY as a hat be inspired by the Industrial Revolution? If you have followed Norah Gaughan's career, the answer is a snorted and adamant yes.

For Norah, it is a short leap from the wrought-iron pylons, girders, and trusses that formed 19th-century engineering marvels, from the 59th Street Bridge to the Eiffel Tower, to the knitted cables on a beret knitted in the round.

It's delightful how clearly Norah's cables evoke the lattice girders of the Eiffel tower; they stand separately at the brim, and join together elegantly at the top. The chart is simplicity itself, and Norah has done the knitter the kindness of shaping the beret from the bottom up, beginning with a cast-on of many stitches. (No fiddling with four twisty little stitches at the start.) One skein of Jill Draper's Windham, a yarn that is beautifully engineered for roundness and a springy twist, and you've got yourself a beret, which in and of itself is a symbol of revolution.

## KNITTED MEASUREMENTS

— Body Circumference: 20" (51 cm) at brim
— Length: 8½" (21.5 cm)

## MATERIALS

— Windham by Jill Draper Makes Stuff [4 oz (113 g) skeins, each approx 220 yds (201 m), 100% US merino wool]: 1 skein Iced Mocha or Merlot
Note: One skein will make one hat, with only a few yards left; it is important to match the gauge so that you do not run out of yarn.
— Size US 7 (4.5 mm) circular needles, 16" (40 cm) and 24" (60 cm) long, and double-pointed needles (set of 4 or 5), or size needed to achieve gauge
— Size US 5 (3.75 mm) circular needle, 16" (40 cm) long.
— Stitch marker
— Cable needle

## GAUGE

20 sts and 28 rows = 4" (10 cm) over stockinette stitch, using larger needle
Note: The fabric may seem heavy and dense, but it is important to get the gauge.

## NOTES

The hat is worked in the round from the bottom up.
Place markers between Cable Pattern repeats to track position in pattern.

# STITCH PATTERNS

## 1×1 RIB

(even number of sts)
— All Rnds: *K1, p1; rep from * to end.

## CABLE PATTERN

(multiple of 28 sts; inc to multiple of 42 sts; dec to multiple of 4 sts)
*Note:* See abbreviations and chart on pages 26–27.

— *Rnd 1:* *P1, k26, p1; rep from * to end.
— *Rnd 2:* *P1, k3, M1L, k7, 3/3 LC, k7, M1R, k3, p1; rep from * to end—30 sts.
— *Rnd 3 and all Odd-Numbered Rnds through Rnd 53:* Knit the knit sts and purl the purl sts as they face you.
— *Rnd 4:* *P1, k3, M1L, k5, 3/3 RPC, 3/3 LPC, k5, M1R, k3, p1; rep from * to end—32 sts.
— Rnd 6: *P1, k3, M1L, 3/1 LPC, 3/2 RPC, p6, 3/2 LPC, 3/1 RPC, M1R, k3, p1; rep from * to end—34 sts.

- *Rnd 8*: *P1, k3, M1L, k1, p1, 3/1 LPC, k2, p10, k2, 3/1 RPC, p1, k1, M1R, k3, p1; rep from * to end—36 sts.
- *Rnd 10*: *P1, k3, M1L, k2, p2, 3/2 LPC, p10, 3/2 RPC, p2, k2, M1R, k3, p1; rep from * to end—38 sts.
- *Rnd 12*: *P1, k3, M1L, 3/1 LC, p3, 3/2 LPC, p6, 3/2 RPC, p3, 3/1 RC, M1R, k3, p1; rep from * to end—40 sts.
- *Rnd 14*: *P1, k3, M1L, k5, p5, 3/3 LPC, 3/3 RPC, p5, k5, M1R, k3, p1; rep from * to end—42 sts.
- *Rnd 16*: *P1, k6, 3/1 LPC, p7, 3/3 LC, p7, 3/1 RPC, k6, p1; rep from * to end.
- *Rnd 18*: *P1, k5, ssk, 3/1 LPC, p3, 3/3 RPC, 3/3 LPC, p3, 3/1 RPC, k2tog, k5, p1—40 sts.
- *Rnd 20*: *P1, k6, p1, 3/1 LPC, 3/2 RPC, p6, 3/2 LPC, 3/1 RPC, p1, k6, p1; rep from * to end.
- *Rnd 22*: *P1, k5, ssk, p1, 3/1 LPC, k2, p10, k2, 3/1 RPC, p1, k2tog, k5, p1; rep from * to end—38 sts.
- *Rnd 24*: *P1, k6, p2, 3/2 LPC, p10, 3/2 RPC, p2, k6, p1; rep from * to end.
- *Rnd 26*: *P1, k5, ssk, p3, 3/2 LPC, p6, 3/2 RPC, p3, k2tog, k5, p1; rep from * to end—36 sts.
- *Rnd 28*: *P1, k6, p5, 3/3 LPC, 3/3 RPC, p5, k6, p1; rep from * to end.

- *Rnd 30*: *P1, k5, ssk, p7, 3/3 LC, p7, k2tog, k5, p1; rep from * to end— 34 sts.
- *Rnd 32*: *P1, k3, 3/1 LPC, p3, 3/3 RPC, 3/3 LPC, p3, 3/1 RPC, k3, p1; rep from * to end.
- *Rnd 34*: *P1, k2, ssk, 3/1 LPC, 3/2 RPC, p6, 3/2 LPC, 3/1 RPC, k2tog, k2, p1; rep from * to end—32 sts.
- *Rnd 36*: *P1, k3, p1, 3/1 LPC, k2, p10, k2, 3/1 RPC, p1, k3, p1; rep from * to end.
- *Rnd 38*: *P1, k2, ssk, p1, 3/2 LPC, p10, 3/2 RPC, p1, k2tog, k2, p1; rep from * to end—30 sts.
- *Rnd 40*: *P1, k3, p3, 3/2 LPC, p6, 3/2 RPC, p3, k3, p1; rep from * to end.
- *Rnd 42*: *P1, k2, ssk, p4, 3/3 LPC, 3/3 RPC, p4, k2tog, k2, p1; rep from * to end—28 sts.
- *Rnd 44*: *P1, k3, p7, 3/3 LC, p7, k3, p1; rep from * to end.
- *Rnd 46*: *P1, k2, ssk, p3, 3/3 RPC, 3/3 LPC, p3, k2tog, k2, p1; rep from * to end—26 sts.
- *Rnd 48*: *P1, k2, ssk, 3/2 RPC, p6, 3/2 LPC, k2tog, k2, p1; rep from * to end—24 sts.
- *Rnd 50*: *P1, k2, ssk, k2, p10, k2, k2tog, k2, p1; rep from * to end— 22 sts.

- *Rnd 52*: *P1, k2, ssk, k1, p10, k1, k2tog, k2, p1; rep from * to end—20 sts.
- *Rnd 54*: *P1, k2, ssk, p10, k2tog, k2, p1; rep from * to end—18 sts.
- *Rnd 55*: *P1, k2, ssk, p8, k2tog, k2, p1; rep from * to end—16 sts.
- *Rnd 56*: *P1, k2, ssk, p6, k2tog, k2, p1; rep from * to end—14 sts.
- *Rnd 57*: *P1, k2, ssk, p4, k2tog, k2, p1; rep from * to end—12 sts.
- *Rnd 58*: *P1, k2, ssk, p2, k2tog, k2, p1; rep from * to end—10 sts.
- *Rnd 59*: *P1, k2, ssk, k2tog, k2, p1; rep from * to end—8 sts.
- *Rnd 60*: *P1, k1, ssk, k2tog, k1, p1; rep from * to end—6 sts.
- *Rnd 61*: P1, ssk, k2tog, p1; rep from * to end—4 sts.

*Note*: Change to 24" (60 cm) long circular needle, then to dpns when necessary for number of sts on needle.
- Work Rnds 1–61 of Cable Pattern—20 sts.
- *Dec Rnd 1*: [K3tog] 6 times, k2—8 sts.
- *Dec Rnd 2*: [K2tog] 4 times—4 sts.
- *I-Cord*: K4, slide sts to opposite end of needle so that yarn is coming from left end of sts. *K4, bringing yarn tightly across back of sts; rep from * until i-cord measures 1" (2.5 cm). Cut yarn, leaving 6" (15 cm) tail; thread tail through rem sts, pull tight, and fasten off.

### FINISHING
Weave in ends; block as desired.

## HAT
Using smaller 16" (40 cm) long circular needle and long-tail CO, CO 112 sts. Join, being careful not to twist sts; pm for beg of rnd and work in the rnd as follows:
- Work in 1×1 Rib for 1" (2.5 cm).
- Change to larger 16" (40 cm) long circular needle.
- *Inc Rnd*: *K4, M1L; rep from * to end—140 sts.

## IRONWORKS BERET CHART & ABBREVIATION GUIDE

**3/1 LC (3 over 1 Left Cross)**: Slip the next 3 sts to cn and hold at front of work, k1, k3 from cn.

**3/1 LPC (3 over 1 Left Purl Cross)**: Slip the next 3 sts to cn and hold at front of work, p1, k3 from cn.

**3/1 RC (3 over 1 Right Cross)**: Slip the next st to cn and hold at back of work, k3, k1 from cn.

**3/1 RPC (3 over 1 Right Purl Cross)**: Slip the next st to cn and hold at back of work, k3, p1 from cn.

**3/2 LPC (3 over 2 Left Purl Cross)**: Slip the next 3 sts to cn and hold at front of work, p2, k3 from cn.

**3/2 RPC (3 over 2 Right Purl Cross)**: Slip the next 2 sts to cn and hold at back of work, k3, p2 from cn.

**3/3 LC (3 over 3 Left Cross)**: Slip the next 3 sts to cn and hold at front of work, k3, k3 from cn.

**3/3 LPC (3 over 3 Left Purl Cross)**: Slip the next 3 sts to cn and hold at front of work, p3, k3 from cn.

**3/3 RC (3 over 3 Right Cross)**: Slip the next 3 sts to cn and hold at back of work, k3, k3 from cn.

**3/3 RPC (3 over 3 Right Purl Cross)**: Slip the next 3 sts to cn and hold at back of work, k3, p3 from cn.

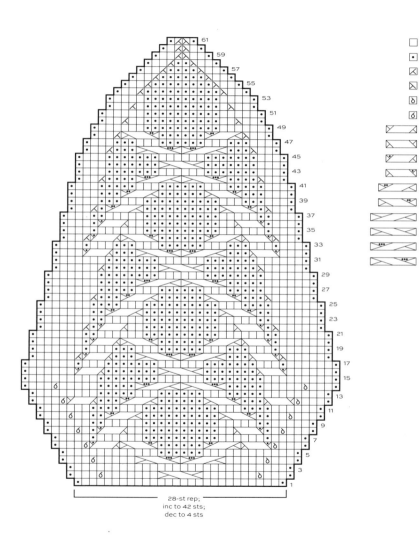

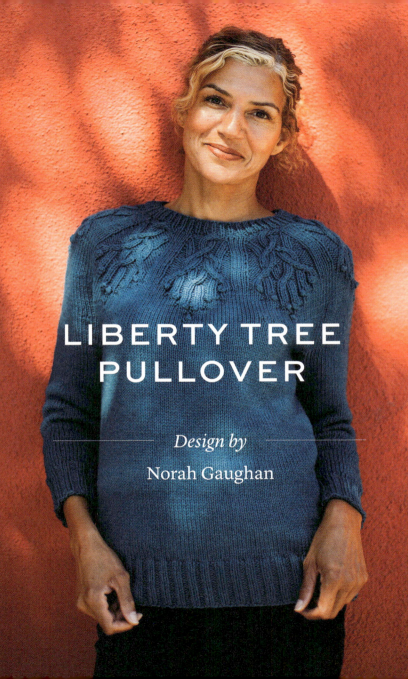

# LIBERTY TREE PULLOVER

*Design by*

Norah Gaughan

REVOLUTIONS START WITH AN IDEA, but they also come to life in very real places. Consider, for example, the American Revolution. It had to start somewhere, right? Well, it was an elm tree in Boston Common that marked the location of the first public protest against the British government's Stamp Act in 1765.

This towering tree quickly became a gathering place for protests, a billboard of sorts where calls to action were posted, a rallying point. When the Stamp Act was repealed the following year, the Liberty Tree was the site of the celebration, with streamers and lanterns all over its branches.

It became a potent symbol of what the colonists craved so desperately. When word spread of the Liberty Tree in Boston Common, other cities across the colonies named their own Liberty Trees. Of course, the British Army cut down this symbol of protest and freedom in 1775. That'll show 'em, they figured.

A tree makes for a beautiful cable pattern, just saying. And for Norah Gaughan to be thinking about the Liberty Tree as she designed this pullover, well, it gives us plenty to think about as we knit it.

Norah chose Spud 'n' Chloe Sweater, a wool and cotton blend that we really love, for this timeless garment.

## KNITTED MEASUREMENTS

— Bust: 32 (36, 40, 44, 48, 52, 56)"
  [81.5 (91.5, 101.5, 112, 122, 132, 142) cm]
— Length: 25 (26, 26½, 27½, 28, 29,
  29½)" [63.5 (66, 67.5, 70, 71, 73.5,
  75) cm

## SIZES

To fit bust sizes 28–30 (32–34, 36–38,
40–42, 44–46, 48–50, 52–54)" [71–76
(81.5–86.5, 91.5–96.5, 101.5–106.5,
112–117, 122–127, 132–137) cm]

## MATERIALS

— Sweater by Spud & Chloë [100 g
  skeins, each approx 160 yds (146 m),
  55% superwash wool / 45%
  certified organic cotton]: 6 (6, 7, 8,
  9, 10, 10) skeins Moonlight
— Size US 6 (4 mm) circular needles,
  16" (40 cm) and 24" (60 cm) long or
  longer, and double-pointed needles
  (set of 4 or 5), or size needed to
  achieve gauge
— Size US 4 (3.5 mm) circular needles,
  16" (40 cm) and 24" (60 cm) long or
  longer, and double-pointed needles
  (set of 4 or 5)
— Stitch markers
— Cable needle
— Waste yarn

## GAUGE

20 sts and 28 rows = 4" (10 cm) over
stockinette stitch, using larger needle

## NOTES

Pullover worked in rnd from top down to
armholes; sleeves and body are divided
and worked separately in rnd to bottom
edge. Short rows shape back neck.
Place markers between Cable Pattern
repeats to track position in pattern.

# CABLE PATTERN

(multiple of 14 sts; inc to multiple of 28 sts)
*Note:* See abbreviations and chart on
pages 36–37.

— *Rnd 1:* *K2, [p2, k2] 3 times; rep from
  * to end.
— *Rnd 2 and all Even-Numbered Rnds:*
  Knit the knit sts and purl the purl sts
  as they face you.
— *Rnd 3:* *K2, M1L, p2, 2/2/2 RPC, p2,
  M1R, k2; rep from * to end—16 sts.
— *Rnd 5:* *K2, M1L, k1, p2, [k2, p2]
  twice, k1, M1R, k2; rep from * to
  end—18 sts.
— *Rnd 7:* *K2, M1PL, k2, [p2, k2] 3
  times, M1PR, k2; rep from * to
  end—20 sts.

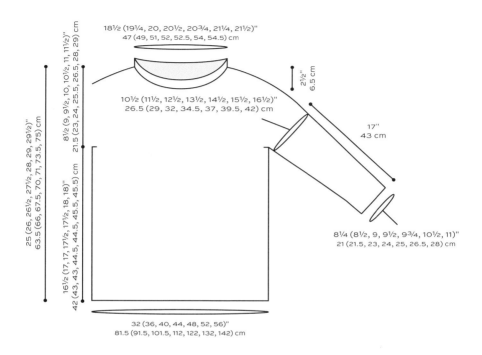

- *Rnd 9*: *K2, M1PL, p1, k2, [p2, k2] 3 times, p1, M1PR, k2; rep from * to end—22 sts.
- *Rnd 11*: *K2, M1PL, p2, k2, p2, 2/2/2 RPC, p2, k2, p2, M1PR, k2; rep from * to end—24 sts.
- *Rnd 13*: *K2, p3, k2, 2/2 RC, p2, 2/2 LC, k2, p3, k2; rep from * to end.
- *Rnd 15*: *K2, M1PL, p3, 2/2 RPC, k2, p2, k2, 2/2 LPC, p3, M1PR, k2; rep from * to end—26 sts.
- *Rnd 17*: Rep Rnd 2.
- *Rnd 19*: *K2, M1PL, p4, k2, 2/2 RC, p2, 2/2 LC, k2, p4, M1PR, k2; rep from * to end—28 sts.
- *Rnd 21*: *K2, p5, 2/2 RPC, k2, p2, k2, 2/2 LPC, p5, k2; rep from * to end.
- *Rnd 23*: *K2, p3, 2/2 RC, p2, [k2, p2] twice, 2/2 LC, p3, k2; rep from * to end.
- *Rnd 25*: *K2, p1, 2/2 RPC, k2, [p2, k2] 3 times, 2/2 LPC, p1, k2; rep from * to end.

- *Rnd 27*: *K2, p1, [k2, p2] twice, 2/2/2 RPC, [p2, k2] twice, p1, k2; rep from * to end.
- *Rnd 29*: *K4, MB, p2, [k2, p2] 4 times, MB, k4; rep from * to end.
- *Rnd 31*: Rep Rnd 2.
- *Rnd 33*: *K8, MB, p2, [k2, p2] twice, MB, k8; rep from * to end.
- *Rnd 35*: Rep Rnd 2.
- *Rnd 37*: *K12, MB, p2, MB, k12; rep from * to end.
- *Rnd 39*: Knit.
- *Rnd 41*: *K13, SB, k13; rep from * to end.

## 2×2 RIB
(multiple of 4 sts)
- *All Rnds*: *K2, p2; rep from * to end.

## 1×1 RIB
(even number of sts)
- *All Rnds:* *K1, p1; rep from * to end.

# YOKE
Using larger 16" (40 cm) long circular needle, CO 98 (112, 126, 140, 154, 168, 182) sts. Join, being careful not to twist sts; pm for beg of rnd and work in the rnd as follows:

*Note*: Change to 24" (60 cm) long circular needle when necessary for number of sts on needle.

- Work Rnds 1–41 of Cable Pattern, working incs as indicated—196 (224, 252, 280, 308, 336, 364) sts. Pm after 56 (56, 84, 84, 112, 112, 140) sts (marker A; this should be between 2 Cable Pattern reps), then pm 84 sts after the first marker (marker B; this should be between 2 Cable Pattern reps); these sts mark the 3 center front Cable Pattern reps. Beg-of-rnd marker should fall somewhere between center and left side of back.
- Change to st st.

## SHAPE BACK NECK
*Note:* Back neck is shaped using German Short Rows (see page 11).
- *Short Row 1 (RS)*: Knit to marker A, turn.
- *Short Row 2 (WS)*: DS, purl past beg-of-rnd marker to marker B, turn.
- *Short Row 3*: DS, knit to DS, close DS, k3, turn.
- *Short Row 4*: DS, purl to DS, close DS, p3, turn.
- *Short Rows 5–18*: Rep Short Rows 3 and 4 seven times.

- *Short Row 19*: DS, knit to DS, close DS, knit to end; do not turn.
- Resume knitting in the rnd (closing DSs as you come to them); remove beg-of-rnd marker, knit to marker A, remove marker, k28, pm, k28, pm for new beginning of rnd. These markers mark the center Cable Pattern rep.
- Remove marker B when you come to it on next rnd.
- *Inc Rnd*: K6 (7, 10, 14, 10, 27, 20), M1L, [k12 (14, 12, 25, 20, 51, 33), M1L] 13 (13, 17, 9, 13, 5, 9) times, knit to end—210 (238, 270, 290, 322, 342, 374) sts.
- Continuing in st st, work even until piece measures 8½ (9, 9½, 10, 10½, 11, 11½)" [21.5 (23, 24, 25.5, 26.5, 28, 29) cm] from highest point.

## BODY
- *Dividing Rnd*: Remove marker, k20 (25, 30, 34, 39, 43, 48), place next 38 (42, 48, 50, 56, 58, 64) sts on waste yarn for right sleeve, CO 6 (6, 6, 7, 7, 8, 8) sts for underarm, pm for new beg of rnd, CO 7 (7, 7, 8, 8, 9, 9) sts for underarm, k67 (77, 87, 95, 105, 113, 123), place next 38 (42, 48,

50, 56, 58, 64) sts on waste yarn for left sleeve, CO 13 (13, 13, 15, 15, 17, 17) sts for underarm, knit to beg of rnd—160 (180, 200, 220, 240, 260, 280) sts.
- Work in st st until piece measures 13½ (14, 14, 14½, 14½, 15, 15)" [34.5 (35.5, 35.5, 37, 37, 38, 38) cm] from underarm.
- Change to smaller 24" (60 cm) circular needle.
- *Inc Rnd*: *K5, M1L; rep from * to end—192 (216, 240, 264, 288, 312, 336) sts.
- Work in 2×2 Rib for 3" (7.5 cm).
- BO all sts in pattern.

## SLEEVES
- Using larger dpns, and beginning at center underarm, pick up and knit 7 (7, 7, 8, 8, 9, 9) sts from the 6 (6, 6, 7, 7, 8, 8) CO underarm sts, knit across sts from waste yarn, pick up and knit 8 (8, 8, 9, 9, 10, 10) sts from the 7 (7, 7, 8, 8, 9, 9) CO underarm sts—53 (57, 63, 67, 73, 77, 83) sts; place marker for beginning of rnd and work in the round as follows:
- Knit 14 (12, 10, 10, 8, 8, 6) rnds.

## SHAPE SLEEVE

- *Dec Rnd*: K2, k2tog, knit to last 4 sts, ssk, k2—2 sts dec.
- Rep Dec Rnd every 14 (12, 10, 10, 8, 8, 6) rnds 5 (6, 5, 1, 5, 5, 13) more time(s), then every 0 (0, 8, 8, 6, 6, 0) rnds 0 (0, 3, 8, 6, 6, 0) times—41 (43, 45, 47, 49, 53, 55) sts.
- Work even until piece measures 14" (35.5 cm) from underarm, or to 3" (7.5 cm) less than desired length, inc 3 (1, 3, 1, 3, 3, 1) st(s) evenly on last rnd—44 (44, 48, 48, 52, 56, 56) sts.
- Change to smaller dpns.
- Work in 2×2 Rib for 3" (7.5 cm).
- BO all sts in pattern.

## FINISHING

### Neckband

- Using smaller 16" (40 cm) long circular needle, and beg at center back neck, pick up and knit 92 (96, 100, 102, 104, 106, 108) sts around CO edge [approx 13 (12, 11, 10, 9, 9, 8) sts per Cable pattern rep].
- Work in 1×1 Rib for 1" (2.5 cm).
- BO all sts in pattern.
- Weave in ends; block as desired.

## LIBERTY TREE PULLOVER CHART & ABBREVIATION GUIDE

**2/2 LC (2 over 2 Left Cross)**: Slip the next 2 sts to cn and hold at front of work, k2, k2 from cn.

**2/2 LPC (2 over 2 Left Purl Cross)**: Slip the next 2 sts to cn and hold at front of work, p2, k2 from cn.

**2/2 RC (2 over 2 Right Cross)**: Slip the next 2 sts to cn and hold at back of work, k2, k2 from cn.

**2/2 RPC (2 over 2 Right Purl Cross)**: Slip the next 2 sts to cn and hold at back of work, k2, p2 from cn.

**2/2/2 RPC (2 over 2 over 2 Right Purl Cross)**: Slip the next 4 sts to cn and hold at back of work, k2, slip the last 2 sts from cn to left needle, p2, k2 from cn.

**MB (Make Bobble)**: (K1, yo, k1, yo, k1) into next st, slip these 5 sts back to left needle, k5, slip second, third, fourth, and fifth sts over first st.

**SB (Special Bobble)**: (K2tog, yo, k2tog, yo, k2tog) into next 2 sts, slip these 5 sts back to left needle, k5, slip third, fourth, and fifth sts over first and second sts.

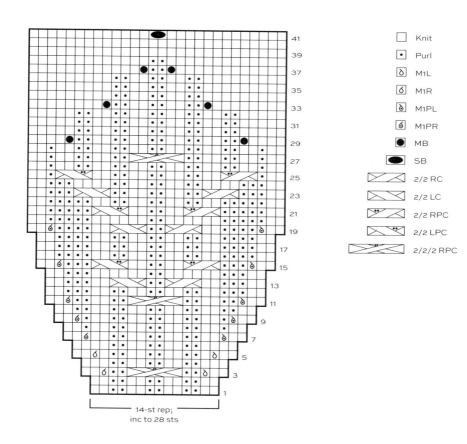

"Hope" is the thing with feathers -
That perches in the soul -
And sings the tune without the words -
And never stops - at all -

And sweetest - in the Gale - is heard
And sore must be the storm -
That could abash the little Bird
That kept so many warm -

I've heard it in the chillest land -
And on the strangest Sea -
Yet - never - in Extremity,
It asked a crumb - of me.


EMILY DICKINSON

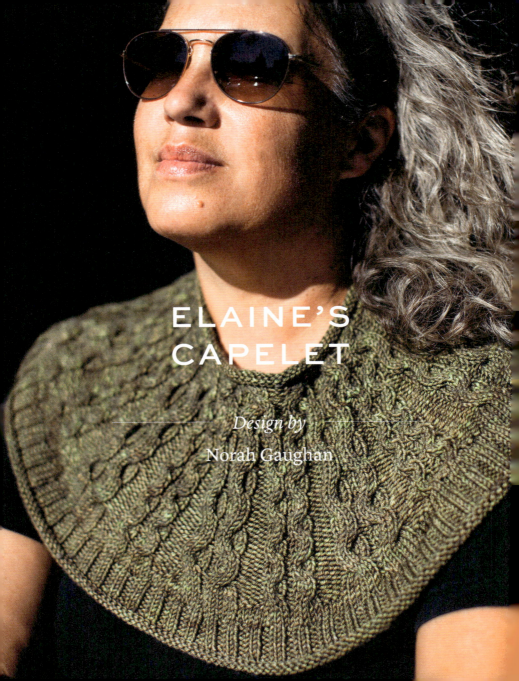

ONE OF MY FAVORITE Seinfeld plotlines involves Elaine's idea for a business that sells just the tops of muffins, leaving the "muffin stumps" behind. The muffin top metaphor resonates so strongly that I apply it here, despite the other connotation of "muffin top," which I resent (and also resemble).

The yoke is the tastiest part of knitting a yoke sweater in the round. If we are knitting the sweater from the bottom up, we gnaw our way through the rounds of plain knitting, chewing stockinette for hours and days, nearly (but not quite) spoiling our appetite for the delicious yoke and its crunchy streusel of cables, texture, or colorwork. If the sweater is top-down, the fun is over after the yoke, and we are left to chew, chew, chew to finish the sweater.

Norah overthrows the whole problem in this project, dumping the muffin stump altogether. We proudly present the world's first yoke sweater that is all yoke and no sweater. It happens to be a versatile addition to any wardrobe, and a gift that is sure to fit.

—Kay

## KNITTED MEASUREMENTS

— Circumference at neck edge: 18¼
  (19¼, 19¾, 20, 20½, 20¾, 21¼)"
  [46.5 (49, 50, 51, 52, 52.5, 54) cm]
— Circumference at bottom edge: 42
  (47½, 54, 58, 64½, 68½, 74¾)"
  [106.5 (120.5, 137, 147.5, 164, 174,
  190) cm]
— Length: 8 (8½, 9, 9½, 10, 10½, 11)"
  [20.5 (21.5, 23, 24, 25.5, 26.5, 28) cm]

## SIZE

To fit bust sizes 32 (36, 40, 44, 48, 52, 56)"
[81.5 (91.5, 101.5, 112, 122, 132, 142) cm]

## MATERIALS

— Julie Asselin Hektos [4 oz (115 g)
  skeins, each approx 200 yds (183 m),
  75% merino wool / 15% cashmere /
  10% silk]: 2 (2, 3, 3, 3, 4, 4) skeins
  Biscotti or Sherwood
— Size US 7 (4.5 mm) circular needles,
  16" (40 cm) and 24" (60 cm) long
— Size US 3 (3.75 mm) circular needles,
  16" (40 cm) and 24" (60 cm) long
— Stitch marker
— Cable needle

## GAUGE

20 sts and 28 rows = 4" (10 cm) over
stockinette stitch, using larger needle

## NOTES

The capelet is worked in the round from
the top down.
Place markers between Cable Pattern
repeats to track position in pattern.

## STITCH PATTERNS

### 2×2 RIB
(multiple of 4 sts)
— All Rnds: *K2, p2; rep from * to end.

### CABLE PATTERN
(multiple of 14 sts; inc to multiple of
28 sts)
*Note:* See abbreviations and chart on
pages 46–47.

— *Rnd 1:* *K6, p1; rep from * to end.
— *Rnd 2:* *3/3 LC, p1, 3/3 RC, p1; rep
  from * to end.
— *Rnd 3 and all Odd-Numbered Rnds:*
  Knit the knit sts and purl the purl sts
  as they face you.
— *Rnd 4:* *K3, M1L, k3, p1, k3, M1R, k3,
  p1; rep from * to end—16 sts.
— *Rnd 6:* *K3, M1L, 2/2 LC, p1, 2/2 RC,
  M1R, k3, p1; rep from * to end—18 sts.
— *Rnd 8:* *3/3 RC, M1L, k2, p1, k2, M1R,
  3/3 LC, p1; rep from * to end—20 sts.

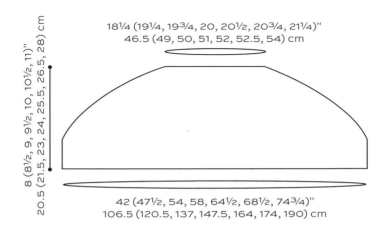

- *Rnd 10*: *K3, M1L, k2, 2/2 RC, p1, 2/2 LC, k2, M1R, k3, p1; rep from * to end—22 sts.
- *Rnd 12*: *K6, M1PL, k4, p1, k4, M1PR, k6, p1; rep from * to end—24 sts.
- *Rnd 14*: *3/3 LC, p1, 2/2 LC, p1, 2/2 RC, p1, 3/3 RC, p1; rep from * to end.
- *Rnd 16*: *K6, M1PL, p1, [k4, p1] twice, M1PR, k6, p1; rep from * to end—26 sts.
- *Rnd 18*: *K6, p2, 2/2 RC, p1, 2/2 LC, p2, k6, p1; rep from * to end.
- *Rnd 20*: *3/3 RC, M1PL, p2, k4, p1, k4, p2, M1PR, 3/3 LC, p1; rep from * to end—28 sts.
- *Rnd 22*: *K6, p3, 2/2 LC, p1, 2/2 RC, p3, k6, p1; rep from * to end.
- *Rnd 24*: Rep Rnd 3.
- *Rnd 26*: *3/3 LC, p3, 2/2 RC, p1, 2/2 LC, p3, 3/3 RC, p1; rep from * to end.
- *Rnd 28*: Rep Rnd 3.
- *Rnd 30*: Rep Rnd 22.
- *Rnd 32*: *3/3 RC, p3, k4, p1, k4, p3, 3/3 LC, p1; rep from * to end.
- *Rnd 34*: *K6, p3, 2/2 RC, p1, 2/2 LC, p3, k6, p1; rep from * to end.
- *Rnd 36*: Rep Rnd 3.
- *Rnd 38*: *3/3 LC, p3, 2/2 LC, p1, 2/2 RC, p3, 3/3 LC, p1; rep from * to end.
- *Rnd 40*: Rep Rnd 3.
- *Rnd 42*: Rep Rnd 34.
- *Rnd 44*: Rep Rnd 32.
- *Rnd 46*: Rep Rnd 22.
- *Rnd 47*: Rep Rnd 3.

## CAPELET

Using larger 16" (40 cm) long circular needle, CO 98 (112, 126, 140, 154, 168, 182) sts. Join, being careful not to twist sts; pm for beg of rnd and work in the rnd as follows:

*Note*: Change to 24" (60 cm) long circular needle when necessary for number of sts on needle.

— Work Rnds 1–47 of Cable Pattern, working incs as indicated—196 (224, 252, 280, 308, 336, 364) sts.
— *Inc Rnd*: \*K14 (16, 14, 28, 22, 56, 36), M1L; rep from \* to last 0 (0, 0, 0, 0, 0, 4) sts, knit to end—210 (238, 270, 290, 322, 342, 374) sts.
— Change to st st; work even until piece measures 6½ (7, 7½, 8, 8½, 9, 9½)" [16.5 (18, 19, 20.5, 21.5, 23, 24) cm].
— Change to smaller 24" (60 cm) long circular needle.
— *Inc Rnd*: \*K5, M1L; rep from \* to last 0 (8, 0, 0, 12, 12, 4) sts, knit to end—252 (284, 324, 348, 384, 408, 448) sts.
— Work in 2×2 Rib for 1" (2.5 cm).
— *Dec Rnd*: \*K5, k2tog; rep from \* to last 0 (4, 2, 12, 6, 2, 0) sts, knit to end—216 (244, 278, 300, 330, 350, 384) sts.
— Knit 2 rnds.
— BO all sts.

## FINISHING

### Neckband

Using smaller 16" (40 cm) long circular needle, pick up and knit 91 (96, 99, 100, 102, 104, 106) sts around neck [approx 13 (12, 11, 10, 9, 9, 8) sts in each Cable Pattern rep]. Pm for beg of rnd and work in the rnd as follows:

— Work in st st for 1" (2.5 cm).
— BO all sts.
— Weave in ends; block as desired.

46

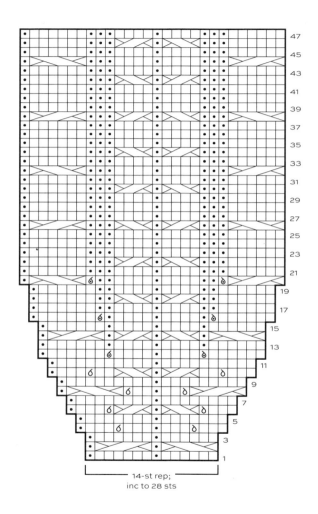

## ELAINE'S CAPELET CHART & ABBREVIATION GUIDE

**2/2 LC (2 over 2 Left Cross)**: Slip the next 2 sts to cable needle and hold at front of work, k2, k2 from cable needle.

**2/2 RC (2 over 2 Right Cross)**: Slip the next 2 sts to cable needle and hold at back of work, k2, k2 from cable needle.

**3/3 LC (3 over 3 Left Cross)**: Slip the next 3 sts to cable needle and hold at front of work, k3, k3 from cable needle.

**3/3 RC (3 over 3 Right Cross)**: Slip the next 3 sts to cable needle and hold at back of work, k3, k3 from cable needle.

## GETTING TO KNOW DESIGNER NORAH GAUGHAN

Working with Norah Gaughan is a dream come true for us. We have been admiring—and making—her designs for nearly as long as we have been knitting. Although she can design almost anything, she is best known for innovative construction and textural work, especially cables. She is the author of several books, including *Knitting Nature* and *Norah Gaughan's Knitted Cable Sourcebook*.

At the same time as this Field Guide, Norah is publishing a new collection of designs with interchangeable cables as well as instructions and a worksheet for customizing details, such as gauge, silhouette, and sleeve style. The cables she designed for the three sweaters presented here are interchangeable with the ones in that collection, suitably called *Interchange*, so we encourage you to check it out on her website: norahgaughan.com.

**You have been knitting for most of your life and designing knitwear professionally for more than 30 years. What keeps you going?**
There is always something new to learn or make up or do in a different way.

**Once we introduced the theme of Revolution, how did you begin designing?**
I started by searching for symbols of revolution on Pinterest and Google and making a visual idea board that included atoms (scientific revolution), peace symbols and doves (anti-war revolution), bridges (industrial revolution), and an engraving showing the liberty tree (a symbol of the American Revolution).

I also had a lot of fun thinking about the multiple meanings of the word "revolution": knit in the round (one round is a revolution); a round shape (each cable has some roundness to it); something new; and a fight for a cause we believe in.

**What was your favorite part of working on this Field Guide?**
My favorite part was making up the new, interchangeable cables and, at the same time, getting them to fit into the required shape and gracefully transition into the stockinette stitch body.

I especially love how the sinuous lines of the Calligraphy Cardigan cable curve toward each other to form a point; this allows the reverse stockinette stitch background of the yoke to be separated from the stockinette stitch background of the body. I was pleased when I realized that the Liberty Tree cable pattern could transition into stockinette stitch by ending the rib along a diagonal line, which is the framework for the pointed ending, punctuated with little bobbles. (The bobbles are included in the written instructions and on the chart, but they are definitely optional.)

**In the *Knitted Cable Sourcebook*, you shared your process for designing new cables, which seems to be a mix of doodling, geometry, and logical progressions. How did the cables in this Field Guide evolve?**
All of them are new progressions of previous work. For Calligraphy I expanded Stable Twist (#61) from the *Knitted Cable Sourcebook* to encompass a larger cable twist in the center; I also extended the cross lines. For Ironworks, I explored ways of connecting sinuous lines, which for me is a lot like drawing. I examine something similar in Bulb (#144) in my book. Liberty Tree is a new variation of Weeping Blossom (#114), re-engineered to be worked from the top down and to transition easily into the stockinette stitch body of the sweater. For Elaine's Capelet, I merged two sizes of O cables (the hugs of the well-known OXO hugs and kisses cable) in a new way.

**Next up?**
I've become fascinated with twisted stitches, and I am starting to explore methods for teaching knitters how to make up their own.

**Count us in!**

## ABBREVIATIONS

**Approx:** Approximately

**Beg:** Begin(ning)(s)

**BO:** Bind off

**Cn:** Cable needle

**CO:** Cast on

**Dec:** Decreas(ed)(es)(ing)

**Dpn:** Double-pointed needle(s)

**DS:** Double stitch (see German Short Rows, page 11).

**Inc:** Increas(ed)(es)(ing)

**Kfb:** Knit into the front and back of the next stitch. One stitch has been increased.

**K2tog:** Knit 2 stitches together. One stitch has been decreased.

**K3tog:** Knit 3 stitches together. Two stitches have been decreased.

**K:** Knit

**M1L:** (make 1 left) Insert left needle from front to back under horizontal strand between stitch just worked and the next stitch on the left needle. Knit this strand through the back loop. One stitch has been increased.

**M1PL:** (make 1 purlwise, left) Insert left needle from front to back under horizontal strand between stitch just worked and the next stitch on the left needle. Purl this strand through the back loop. One stitch has been increased.

**M1PR:** (make 1 purlwise, right) Insert left needle from back to front under horizontal strand between stitch just worked and the next stitch on the left needle. Purl this strand through the front loop. One stitch has been increased.

**M1R:** (make 1 right) Insert left needle from back to front under horizontal strand between stitch just worked and the next stitch on the left needle. Knit this strand through the front loop. One stitch has been increased.

**P2tog:** Purl 2 stitches together. One stitch has been decreased.

**P:** Purl

| | |
|---|---|
| **Pfb:** | Purl into the front and back of the next stitch. One stitch has been increased. |
| **Pm:** | Place marker |
| **Rep:** | Repeat(ed)(ing)(s) |
| **Rnd(s):** | Round(s) |
| **RS:** | Right side |
| **Sl:** | Slip |
| **Sm:** | Slip marker |
| **Ssk:** | Slip 1 stitch knitwise, slip 1 stitch purlwise, insert left needle into the front of these 2 stitches and knit them together from this position. One stitch has been decreased. |
| **St st:** | stockinette stitch |
| **St(s):** | Stitch(es) |
| **Tbl:** | Through the back loop(s) |
| **Tog:** | Together |
| **WS:** | Wrong side |

# A DAILY DOSE OF MDK

Psst. Hey, you. You reading this Field Guide. Do you know that in addition to producing this precious little book (and all the Field Guides), Mason-Dixon Knitting is a daily magazine on the internet? Every day, Ann and Kay and a stellar cast of contributors scan the globe for the best in knitting, and about knitting. It's a daily dose of beauty, encouragement, instruction, and laughs.

Someone recently called Mason-Dixon Knitting "the grand stage of knitting," and we had to go lie down for a while.

Mason-Dixon Knitting is the knitting website that we have always wished for, so we made it.

Mason-Dixon Knitting is also a shop, where we bring you special yarns made by special people, including all of the yarns that you see knitted up in this Field Guide.

Mason-Dixon Knitting also has a Lounge, where knitters virtually gather to get how-to answers, to organize themselves for charity knitting projects and real-life knitting adventures, and to goof off.

Mason-Dixon Knitting is a haven, and a heaven, for knitters. We're there every morning, bright and early, holding up something new.